The Soil of Salvation:
An Advent Journey with Isaiah

By
Dwain Cassady

Also available from Dwain Cassady:

**Insights from Matthew:
An Advent Journey**

**The Coming Light:
An Advent Journey with John**

**Presence in the Manger:
An Advent Journey with Luke**

Unless otherwise indicated, all scripture references
are from the New Revised Standard Version, 1989.

Opening

Taken and broken life slips through
Fingers clinched hard tight
Grasping, gripping, clinging, holding
To own do I fight.

Wanting and needing do I strive
With all of my strength
To possess and hold and control
I'll go any length.

Farther and faster life does run
So I grip stronger
The fight begun already lost
Can't hold much longer.

Fingers weakened weary open
All sought surely lost
I cringe despair as I lose grip
Couldn't pay the cost.

Clinching fists open to release
Even as I plead
I can't I can't I can't I can't
Grasp that which I need.

Expecting all is total loss
My eyes I do peek
To see grace coming towards me
Gifting what I seek.

What I crushed grasping freely comes
After I release
And opening my heart and hands
Receive gifted peace.

With heart felt joy I discover
That I wished to hold
Comes so abundantly given
By one Love so bold.

-Dwain Cassady

Table of Contents

6

To the Reader

Out of angst and anguish the prophet, somehow, is able to discern the one thread that, with God's hand, will move the world forward on the path to wholeness. In this book, we will eavesdrop on those marvelous texts that arose from the great vision in Isaiah, words that provide the very soil out of which our salvation grows. The prophets were able to see hope where there was only despair, possibility where there were only dead ends, and the telos for how God's loving nurture of the world would combine with human history to result in renewed hope and life. It is my hope that as you journey through this Advent season with these jewels from Isaiah you will not only see how God loved us so much that God sent Jesus to be born, but also discern how the love of God will move you forward from anguish into abundant life.

There are 29 devotionals in this book to accommodate the longest Advent season we can have, which is when Christmas falls on Sunday. If Christmas falls on a day other than Sunday, I recommend you start the daily devotionals before the first Sunday of Advent, 6 days early if Christmas is on Monday, 5 days early if Christmas is on Tuesday, etc., so that you will end up with the Christmas Day devotional on Christmas Day.

8

The Coming Presence
Isa. 64:1-4

"O that you would tear open the heavens and come down, so that the mountains would quake at your presence." (Isa. 64:1) Advent is a season of longing, yearning, waiting for God to come. It is a time when we are in touch with our brokenness and our need for healing, which causes a sense of desperate longing in our hearts for our Creator. But, Isaiah reminds us that the One for whom we are longing is powerful beyond our understanding. God's presence may be more than we bargained for!

What makes mountains quake? Perhaps earthquakes and volcanos can make mountains shake, but to make a mountain quake implies a sense of fear, as well. God's presence is truly an awe inspiring, overwhelming thing! To me one of the hymns that best captures the sense of awe that surrounds us in the Advent season is "Let All Mortal Flesh Keep Silence." The last line goes, "At his feet the six-winged seraph, cherubim, with sleepless eye, veil their faces to the presence, as with ceaseless voice they cry: Alleluia, Alleluia, Alleluia, Lord Most High!"[1] The holy presence of God is powerful enough to make mountains quake and heavenly beings veil their faces!

Try to sit back, close your eyes, and imagine God as a being who is so powerful as to be able to create this nearly infinite universe in which we live.

Try to picture a being who is great enough, awesome enough, to exist outside and beyond the universe, not just beyond our little planet! Isaiah is inviting, no pleading for, this holy Being to tear open the heavens and come down! What is he thinking? Yet, that is exactly where I stand as I enter Advent: in need of my Creator, no matter how terrible that Presence may be.

I think Isaiah knew the knee weakening disruption for which he was calling when he pleaded for God to come. Isaiah could see that his people had no hope unless God came into their midst. Helpless and floundering in their own ways and solutions, Isaiah's people were lost and had no idea of which way to turn. With dark, heavy hearts, they suffered in a mess of their own making. While people knew in their minds that God was the answer, they thought in their hearts that they could make God do what they wanted God to do, forgetting that God has a mind and will of God's own. Hmmm. Sounds pretty much like today! "O that you would tear open the heavens and come down, so that the mountains would quake at your presence." (Isa. 64:1)

Prayer: Almighty God, creator of the universe, I stand in need of your Presence to reorient my life and heart. Without you I admit that I am lost. Please come to me, Emmanuel. Amen.

Filthy Rags
Isa. 64:5-7

Have you ever felt filthy? I'm not talking about the nasty you get after doing a dirty job, like when I do yard work that involves digging. I usually need to be hosed off before I can even come in the garage! I'm talking about feeling filthy in soul and spirit, the kind of disgust one feels after having done something so wrong that you think it can never be made right. If you have been there, then you can begin to get in touch with what this passage in Isaiah is saying.

After begging God to tear open the heavens and come down, Isaiah looks around and sees the sinfulness of his people and himself. Isaiah describes the people to whom God would come as unclean, as people whose iniquities carry them away from life and love. Isaiah could see that neither he nor his people could stand in the presence of Holy, Almighty God. They are broken, and the holiness of God's presence would blow them away like dry leaves before a howling gale.

This part of Isaiah was most likely written near the end of Israel's exile in Babylon, or possibly at the beginning of Israel's return home under Cyrus of Persia.[2] Isaiah had seen his people beaten down and carried away from their homeland. Isaiah could only attribute this catastrophe to sin, the breaking of relationship with God. The Exile left a dark, heavy stone in the spirit of Israel that might never heal.

Isaiah saw the sin of his people as being so pervasive and entrenched that "all our righteous deeds are like a filthy cloth." (Isa. 64:6) Even the good things people did were tainted, soiled, greasy in the light of God's holiness. Ouch! I usually find that doing something good for someone else makes me feel good, not filthy. It is helpful to have a few good deeds to balance out the rest of my life. But, Isaiah is saying that, as human beings, even the good things we do are filthy in God's presence. We are sin. The only thing we can do about it is to realize it.

Isaiah's insights are not just for the sixth century BCE. As I look toward Jesus' coming birth, I become aware that I, too, stand covered with filthy rags. Just as Isaiah knew that if his people could not grasp that truth then they would not be able to be restored into relationship with God, I have to also realize that if I don't really know who I am, I can't truly welcome Jesus into my life.

Prayer: Dear Holy God, I confess that I am not the person you have called me to be. Please come, anyway. Amen.

The Birth of Hope
Isa. 64:8-9

While sin and brokenness can make life so dark that I can see no way forward, there is hope. When good deeds hang like filthy rags, and I am too tired to try, there is One who can save me. In Isaiah 64:1-9, one discovers the three primary components of the soil of salvation: God, brokenness, and hope.

Many people in the time this passage was written had lost hope. They felt God had withdrawn from them and no longer cared. Beaten and dragged from their homeland to Babylon, what could they do? They felt lost and hopeless.

The prophet who penned these verses was able to see beyond the darkness and despair and find that one thread that led to hope: God could still come. While we are powerless to fix ourselves and unable to crawl out of the darkness, if God comes, if God remembers us, then we could still be saved. The hope that God will come into the midst of the lost people of Israel to save is what gave birth to the expectation of a Messiah. Emmanuel, God with us, is the only way out of sin and brokenness.

Isaiah's plea is that the Potter will once again take up the clay and begin to shape. "O Lord, you are our Father; we are the clay, and you are our potter." (Isa. 64:8) While God shaped us in creating us, the hope is that God will take hold again and begin to reshape our lives into useable vessels.

In this wonderful image of the potter and the clay, I have to remember that I am the clay: stiff, sticky mud. Left to itself, clay is simply dirt. It is only when the potter takes the clay and works the clay that it becomes of value. During the season of Advent, we are reminded that human beings are clay in need of a potter, that we are broken and cannot fix ourselves. It is only in the loving hands of God that we find hope.

The prophet knows that God has acted in the past, which gives rise to the hope that God will come again. God is our Father, and we are God's people. Because God is love, we can trust God to not leave us in the darkness. While we can't find our way to God, God will find a way to us. A Messiah will come to restore, heal, and remold our lives with joy.

We join the prophet this Advent season realizing that we are in darkness and looking for God to come and save us. With eyes straining to see further, we search for the light of God to come and yearn for the feel of the potter's hands on our hearts. Without God we are lost. But, we can count on God's love. Hope is born!

Prayer: Almighty, all loving God, life is sometimes so difficult that I can't handle it alone. Please let me feel the presence of your hands so that I can be assured that you will hold me. Amen.

Rise and Shine!
Isa. 60:1-6

Rise and shine! How many sleepy children have been summoned from the sweet stupor of sleep to face a new day with these words? This is also the prophet's summons to his people. "Arise, shine; for your light has come, and the glory of the Lord has risen upon you." (Isa. 60:1)

These words were addressed to a people in the stupor of oppression. The prophet speaks to a people who had been uprooted and dragged to Babylon, where they had been for some 70 years. Most had no memory of Israel, but they all had stories. There was a longing for the homeland, but many had resigned themselves to being stuck where they were. There was a dull hopelessness that this was as good as it would get, like in those waking moments where one is too groggy to really face the day.

The setting into which this prophet speaks is eerily familiar. Life's dark places often have that same feel of dull hopelessness. Whether I am being oppressed as a people, being beat down by the fists of poverty, or battling my own personal darkness of disease, depression, grief, and on and on, there comes a point when the fight begins to drain out of me. I find myself in a stupor of hopelessness, resigned to the idea that this is as good as life gets. Life gets heavier and heavier. My world shrinks to the most immediate concerns, and as I look out all I see is darkness.

If you haven't been in the dark spot to which Isaiah speaks, then good for you! But, please realize that most of the people around you are all too familiar with that darkness. It is into this dark lethargy of spirit that the words from Isaiah break. Like a battle cry, the prophet calls us to shake off the lethargy, open our eyes wide, and look. While there is darkness all around, can't you see that bright light coming in the distance?! Wake up and see that hope is dawning!

The light of the glory of the Lord is coming into our midst! With the coming of the Lord will be blessings beyond counting! See the light just beginning to shine there in the distance? God will come to bring us home, to set us free, to give us joy, again. There is hope. No matter what the darkness is that surrounds us, God's light will penetrate it. "Then you shall see and be radiant; your heart shall thrill and rejoice." (Isa. 60:5)

The soil of salvation is a mixture of despair and hope, brokenness and promise, coming but not yet. It is this hope and promise that I need to help me fend off the darkness and await the Messiah.

Prayer: Dear Holy God, you are my light and hope. Give me the insight I need to see your light in my darkness, to hear your voice in my brokenness, and to trust that you will come and save. I long to be radiant! Amen.

Good News Afoot
Isa. 61:1-2

The prophet speaks to the despair of his people with words of emancipation. God has given him a message of liberation and hope. There is good news afoot! The chains that have bound people will be broken! The prophet is able to see that God desires more for God's people than sin, darkness, and brokenness. God's gift of life is meant to be precious and joyful, not heavy and burdensome. But, the only way the weight of life can be lifted is by the restoration of our relationship with God.

This is such a seminal passage in the soil of salvation that Jesus picks it as the defining description of his ministry and mission in Luke 4:16-21. It defines the coming Messiah as one who will right the wrongs of our world, who will champion the cause of the least among us, and who will restore all of humanity to a joyful life. The prophet writing in Isaiah was probably thinking in terms of God restoring the people of Israel to their homeland and ending the torture they had been enduring. We now know that the Messianic mission is much greater than the saving of one people. These words of good news are meant for all of humanity!

This can also be a difficult passage for many of us. Do you see yourself in the list of people to be saved? Are you among the oppressed, brokenhearted, captives, and prisoners? We could probably all count ourselves among those who mourn, but as we read through this list we might feel left out. One of the problems with being among the well to do of the world— those who have the financial and personal resources to do life successfully—is that it is easy to think that one is self-sufficient. And, if I can do it, then everyone else should pull themselves up by their bootstraps and do it, too. When people get into this mode of thinking, they tend to lose sight of their neighbors and the struggles other people are having. The sense of self-sufficiency dulls one's perception of the need for a Messiah. Our material satiety can blind us to our spiritual neediness.

Isaiah 61 is a bold statement from a God who loves us and who sees our need, whether we see it or not. God will come to bind us up, set us free, and give us joy so that we can all share in the joy that is life. If we are of the privileged in the world, we have to get ready to open our arms to the rest of humanity as our brothers and sisters. If we are of the oppressed and brokenhearted, then we have to get ready to love those who have had it easier than we have as we are delivered into joy. The Messiah is coming to bring us all into the fold of God's love.

Prayer: Dear loving God, help me to see my need for you. Please set my heart right so that I can welcome with joy all of my brothers and sisters into your fold. Amen.

A Mantle of Praise
Isa. 61:3-4

I am always frantic when I lose something. I bounce between beating myself up for being so careless and searching, searching, and searching. In the early 1970s, I lost a watch. It had a wide leather band with the watch in the middle, surrounded with rivets, or something. I searched and kicked myself, and kicked myself while I was searching. Finally, as it dawned on me that I would not find the watch, the sadness set in. It was such an intense experience that I still remember it today.

Loss is hard, even if it's just a watch. But, when we lose something important, like a loved one, a house, or a job, we can be devastated. Losing a loved one leaves a hole in one's spirit that can never be filled. Most people know the experience of grieving and mourning. We know the hurt, the lethargy, the "it's going to take time," but time doesn't seem to be in a hurry. We can identify with the Israelites to whom the prophet is writing, at least in terms of mourning.

When we are mourning, we know that platitudes don't help. All of the expressions of, "It happened for a reason," "It's for the best," and "This must have been God's plan," usually serve to fuel anger rather than bring comfort. What we need is someone to hold our hand and walk through the darkness with us, someone to not just say that it will be OK but to stay with us long enough for us to see that possibility in our hearts.

The prophet speaks into the dark well of sadness and says that God has anointed him to "provide for those in Zion—to give them a garland instead of ashes, the oil of gladness instead of mourning, the mantle of praise instead of a faint spirit." (Isa. 61:3) Could this be said any more beautifully? The prophet realizes that God knows the people's pain and will act to not only ease the pain, but transform it into joy and praise. Transforming our mourning into joy is one of the missions of the Messiah. The prophet wants people to know that they can count on God to come and pour out the sadness and refill hearts with gladness. As we watch and wait this Advent season, we too can wait expectantly for a garland of joy.

Prayer: Dear tender God, I am grateful that you love me so completely that you will come into the darkness of my heart with your touch of joy. Help me to wait expectantly and be ready for the transformation you are bringing. Amen.

The Gift of Garments
Isa. 61:8-11

The prophet speaks of God's ability to right wrongs and bring restoration. He foresees that God's love of justice, a persistent theme in the Old Testament, will bring forth the uplifting of the downtrodden and healing of the broken. At the time of this prophet's words, the people of Israel were worn out with being downtrodden and all too familiar with injustice. This is good news for a people who had been herded from their homeland against their will. But it is also good news for all who suffer injustice, robbery, or wrongdoing.

When life puts us in a place where we feel beaten down and can't lift ourselves back up, it is good to hear that we have an advocate, a champion, who will go to bat for us. God, with all the power in the universe, is the One who will restore and heal us. The prophet says that we can count on that!

The prophet uses two images to describe God's tender care for humanity. First of all, he describes God as clothing human beings. "I will greatly rejoice in the Lord, my whole being shall exult in my God; for he has clothed me with the garments of salvation, he has covered me with the robe of righteousness." (Isa. 61:10) As a parent clothes a child to face the day, so God will clothe God's children with the garments of salvation and the robe of righteousness. Jesus might have been pulling from this passage when he told of the return of the prodigal son. When the prodigal returned home, unworthy as he was, his father put a robe on him, brought sandals for his feet, and gave him a ring for his finger. (Luke 15:22) It is with the same tender love that God, my heavenly parent and blind to my unworthiness, will clothe me.

The prophet's use of two garments of clothing, the garments of salvation and robe of righteousness, lets me know that God's work of restoration is two-fold. First of all, with the gift of salvation, God will restore me to a position in God's kingdom as one of God's children. The wrongs will be righted, and I will find myself at home. Secondly, God will work within me so that my heart and life bear the fruit of righteousness. Over a lifetime, God will mold me into a more loving and righteous person. This coming salvation is truly something to get excited about!

The second image the prophet uses is that of plants growing out of the earth. Both mysterious and everyday natural, the earth's ability to bring forth life is a symbol of God's ability to work wonders in human lives. If dirt can bring life into existence then surely I can trust almighty God to bring life and joy out of my brokenness! The promise of the coming Messiah is that God will bring forth life, joy, and wholeness from the mess that is my life.

Prayer: Almighty, all loving God, I wait with eagerness the coming of the Messiah and trust you wholly with my life. Amen.

From Desolation to Delight

Isa. 62:1-5

At the time of these writings, Jerusalem laid abandoned and in ruins, forsaken and desolate. But, the prophet could see, just over the horizon, a transformation coming. The time was coming when God would restore the hustle and bustle to Jerusalem. The city would be inhabited, the ruins rebuilt, and it would shine like the dawn. Forsaken and Desolate would be renamed "My Delight Is in Her" and "Married!"

Just like Jerusalem, life can feel like it is named Forsaken and Desolate. There are still a number of closed buildings and convenience stores in Gainesville left over from the consequences of the Great Recession. There can be places like that in the heart, too, places that just won't come alive again. Places that feel empty and dark, alone.

My desolation in the younger years was loneliness. Being an introverted and not very socially adept person, I struggled when I found myself in the huge crowd of people that was Georgia Tech. My dorm room was literally in the stairwell, sealed off from the hallway, which seemed a fitting symbol for how life was going. If I weren't studying or eating, I often found myself lying on the bed staring at the ceiling. Those were dark days. I found comfort in

God, who shared that darkness with me and lead me out of Desolation.

In the beauty of the imagery from Isaiah, I discover the transformation for which I long. There is desolation in the heart that needs fixing, brokenness that needs healing, loneliness that needs a companion. The prophet could see that through the love of God, this transformation was coming! He could see the time when, "as the bridegroom rejoices over the bride, so shall your God rejoice over you." (Isa. 62:5)

During the Advent season, it is good to position one's self to look forward to the coming of God. I look toward Jesus' birth, trusting that Jesus will be the point of transformation for which I long. I wait and anticipate, knowing that, with God's close presence in Jesus Christ, the dark points of desolation in my heart will begin to be filled with light and joy. God will take me from desolation to delight!

Prayer: Dear caring God, thank you so much for coming into my dark and difficult world with your light and joyful presence. Please help the promise of hope take root in my soul so that I can always move toward the wondrous joys of life lived closely with you. Amen.

The Wait
Isa. 62:6-12

The hard part of Advent is that salvation is coming, but not yet. One has to wait. The prophet pictures sentinels posted on the walls of Jerusalem, and their job is to plead for God to come and establish Jerusalem as a great city. The promise is there. God said that God would restore Jerusalem and bring the Israelites home. The Israelites were still in the process of waiting. The promise gives the Israelites the hope they need to hang on in their difficult situation and wait.

Scientists call the human's preferred scenario instant gratification. People tend to like to get a reward immediately for anything done. Parents practice this regularly with children. Everything children do, as long as it is not bad, is followed by immediate and gushing praise. Parents use trinkets as rewards to help motivate children, and woe be unto the parent if the reward is slow in coming! As children grow, they have to learn that they don't get rewards immediately. Often, even most of the time, a person has to be willing to work and then wait to see the results. Generally, human beings learn to do that fairly well.

However, when I get distressed, when I am hurting and anxious, I often fall back to wanting immediate results. I sometimes see prayer more like a vending machine than a relationship. If I just push the right button, say the right words, I will get what I want when I want it. It is discouraging to pray for something and it not happen. I can begin to feel like the sentinels on the walls of Jerusalem, crying out day and night for God to come, day after day after day.

Beth, my wife, has been in a downhill battle with arthritis and kidney failure for over five years, now. I have prayed and prayed and prayed for healing, or at least some measure of relief for her, and things just keep getting worse. There certainly has been no vending machine effect here. It is hard to wait. It is hard to wonder if the answer for which I am looking will ever come. It is hard to be in that situation where all I have is the promise that God will come, God will act, someday. So, what do I do in the meantime?

When I am living out Advent, the period of watching and waiting, I have to keep my eye on the promise while praying in the present. I have discovered that prayer, while not producing the results I want, keeps me connected to God, helps me to trust that God will help carry us through, and gives me strength to wait on the promise. A lot of life is about watching and waiting, learning to trust God in the meantime while hoping for that promised coming when, "See, your salvation comes; his reward is with him, and his recompense before him." (Isa. 62:11) Then we will be called, "The Redeemed of the Lord." (Isa. 62:12)

Prayer: Dear saving God, sometimes I find myself hurting and seeing no way out. It is hard to wait. I pray that you will give me the ability to hope and trust so that I can find that you are with me, even in the midst of the struggle. Amen.

Harnessing the Power of Memory
Isa. 63:7-9

The angst of life is often a product of relationships gone badly. The prophet sees Israel's suffering as resulting from a break down in the relationship between God and the Israelites. They had turned their backs on each other and were no longer in dialogue. Of course, the prophet sees Israel as having sinned against God. But, he also sees God as having turned away from Israel (see Isa. 64:5). Hence, Israel was wrestling both the homesickness and suffering caused by the Exile and the isolation and loneliness of losing God.

The prophet did not see Israel's situation as hopeless, though. He offers a solution here in Isa. 63:7-9: Remember. The prophet calls Israel to look back and remember all that God has done for them in the past. Think back to Abraham, Isaac, and Jacob. Remember Joseph and the famine. Remember Moses and the Exodus. Remember David and the time of prosperity. Remember "in his love and in his pity he redeemed them; he lifted them up and carried them all the days of old." (Isa. 63:9) Remember that "it was no messenger or angel but his **presence** that saved them." (Isa. 63:9. Emphasis added)

Remembering the good is a way to reconnect the heart when it has hardened and turned away.

When feeling distant from God, isolated and alone, or just numb, it can help to think back, to live back into, to remember, the times when you felt closest to God. Remember the mountain tops and the spiritual "Ah hahs!" Remember the song that sent chills through you. Remember when you felt closest to God. These memories help to warm the heart and draw us back to God, who loves us so.

Remembering can help with human relationships, too. When a marriage begins to cool or a close friendship becomes rocky, taking time to think back and remember when we were close can be a spark that relights the fire. In a marriage, try to remember the dating days, how you couldn't stop thinking about the other person or wait to see them again. Remember the good times you've had with a close friend. Memories can give us the impetus to reconnect, to forgive, and to reconcile.

If you have ever lost in love, then Adele is a singer you need to hear. She seems to live in the anguish of a broken heart. But, who wants to be stuck there? In order to heal and move on, we need to remember who we are and whose we are. One may need to remember back past the relationship from which we are trying to recover in order to rediscover the person we were before the damage was done. We may need to remember all the way back to who created us and who loves us more than we can ever imagine!

The prophet knew that memory is a powerful tool. If he could harness it in his people, there was hope. If we can remember the good times and remember from whom we came and to whom we will return, we can harness the power of hope to help us move through the dark times in our lives, as well.

Prayer: Dear ever loving God, you created me and gave me life. You mark me as your own in baptism and place your seal on my heart with your Holy Spirit. Help me to always remember that your love never fails and that you will never forget me.   Amen.

Blooming Deserts?
Isa. 35:1-2

The prophet looked deep into the eyes and souls of his people and saw desert. Dry, lifeless and barren lives had come of being forced to live in Babylon away from Jerusalem. There literally was a desert between the Israelites and their homeland, and it represented the hopelessness of ever finding home. But, the prophet could see change coming. The prophet could see that God would rescue and restore, so he gave them one of the most beautiful images in the Bible: "the desert shall rejoice and blossom; like the crocus it shall blossom abundantly." (Isa. 35:1-2) Not only would the desert not be a barrier, it would become a source of life and beauty!

In his amazing ability to perceive what God is about, the prophet was able to see that God could transform what seemed hopeless, lifeless, and barren into joy, beauty, and life. God would come and not only save, but bring life and joy to places that had never seen them before. God would come and break down the barriers that prevented people from finding their way back to God. That was good news for the Israelites, and it is good news for today's world, too.

Try taking a moment to look deep into your own life and soul. Where are the desert places? What are the problems or issues that have you feeling stuck and hopeless? Now, try picturing those painful, broken aspects of your life in your mind and imagine them being transformed in to life, beauty, and joy. What will the new image be? How will the deserts blossom? How will your life change? The Messiah is coming to do just that in your life!

The birth of Jesus is the event that sets the crocuses to blooming. The coming of Jesus into the world and his demonstration of God's unconditional, never ending love for human beings gives us the hope we need to envision our deserts blossoming. How much better to have a life filled with crocuses than emptiness! How much better to have a God who loves us and walks with us through the dark times of life! It is the abiding, loving presence of God that brings the transformation. When we know we are not alone and abandoned, we can face anything.

The soil of salvation is the darkness, brokenness, and emptiness in our lives. As we discover God's amazing love and learn to trust that love, live in that love, take on that love, and return that love to the world, our deserts bloom, and our lives become beauty. We discover that the hard places have become our strength and a gift we have to offer the world around us.

Prayer: Dear loving God, I trust you to transform my deserts into life. Please come and give me the strength to trust your love so that I can bloom as your creation. Amen.

Journeying Together
Isa. 35:3-7

It is time to get ready to go home! The prophet foresees the journey his people will take to return to Jerusalem. This will be a long and arduous journey. Only the strongest could survive it. It is important to notice that this journey is not about grabbing your things and going, hoping that you are strong enough to make it. Rather, the emphasis is on helping the weak, the lame, and the blind to be ready for the journey, too. The prophet realizes that in life, we journey together.

I am sure that most people can identify with a need for strengthening the knees or having one's eyes opened. Everybody is broken in some way and needs healing. It is good news to hear that when God comes, God will bring the healing each of us needs. But, in the prophet's vision of going home, he also sees the possibility that people will be helping each other. It is not God's job alone to strengthen the weak knees. The prophet envisions the whole community coming together to bind up the weak, lift up the lame, and walk together to make the journey home. If we are to get home, we will have to go together. The truth is that none of us can make it on our own.

In the journey of life, we have to join hands with one another and with God. Life gives us daily opportunities to practice building each other up, binding up broken hearts, and sharing another person's load. As we learn to, and become comfortable with, helping each other along the way, we discover that roads that looked barren and lifeless are teaming with life, "For waters shall break forth in the wilderness and streams in the desert." (Isa. 35:6) As we go through grief and heartache, we will not be alone. God will be with us, but so will our neighbor. As our bodies break with illness, we will not be left behind, but there will be hands to hold and a Holy Spirit within. This is the stuff of life!

The strength of a loving community and a restored relationship with God are what the coming Messiah will bring. As we learn to live into being community and walking with God, we discover what life is really all about. The coming Messiah will tell us to "love one another as I have loved you." (John 15:12) If we want to see deserts bloom and springs of water gushing up everywhere, then we have to journey together with our God and each other along the road of love.

Prayer: Dear God, you long to walk with me along the journey of life. You also long to see me take another's hand and walk together with you. Please work within my heart so that I can learn to live and love and receive the gift of abundant life. Amen.

The Way Home
Isa. 35:8-10

How can we ever get home? Even if we were free to leave, how could we get there? The Israelites must have had anxiety about ever returning to Jerusalem. The prophet answers them with another beautiful image: a highway to home. The prophet foresees that God will make a way, and what a way it will be!

It is easy to feel lost in this world. I often feel like I am in a jungle with trees and vines blocking my view, and I have no idea which way to even start walking to get out. Sometimes the circumstances of life leave me lost. Sometimes, it is the big decisions I have to make. Sometimes, I just feel overwhelmed by the little things. I can relate to the feeling of the Israelites, not being able to see a way forward, not having any idea how to get back home, and feeling like the anguish would never end.

During my twelfth year of pastoring full time, I was battling depression. I had no idea how to find my way out of the misery. The church I was at was known for being hard on its pastors, and they made no exception for me. Finally, I got so miserable that I reached out for help. After some counseling, I decided that the best thing for me to do was to leave the ministry. Then, possibilities began to open up, and I could see the road to a new life forming. God began to open up a new road where there had not been one before, and I found my way out of the misery and on my way home. The funny thing is that the new highway led me by a small church that was just the right fit for me, and I pastored there for 16 years.

The prophet could see that God has the power and care to open up a highway to lead people home. He even describes it as a fool-proof highway on which "no traveler, not even fools, shall go astray." (Isa. 35:8) No matter how far away home may seem or how big the obstacles, God can make a way for each person. God is sending the Messiah to show us just how much God wants to open up possibilities, shelter us with unconditional love, and lead us home. When we stop trying to force our own way and let God open up the possibilities for us, we can find our way home. The "sorrow and sighing shall flee away," (Isa. 35:10) and we will find joy.

Prayer: Dear guiding God, life can be so hard and dark that I feel lost. Help me to trust that I can always turn to you and the people you have placed around me to discover the light. I trust that you will open up the highway I need to lead me back to you. Amen.

Comfort
Isa. 40:1-2

Oh, to hear those words: "Comfort, O comfort my people," (Isa. 40:1) your suffering is over. What a glorious and joyful day that would be! Can you imagine what it would be like for suffering to end in your life, in the lives of all people?

Suffering and struggle seem to be a part of being human. There may be a couple of people who sail through life with ease, but for most folks, life involves a continuous dance with hurt and heartache, stress and struggle, and grind and grief. Would that God would come and bring an end to all of that! But, God doesn't. People keep hurting, people keep dying, and people keep suffering.

The season of Advent positions each of us just like the people to whom the prophet was writing. We are waiting and watching for the Messiah to come, waiting for God to pronounce and end to our suffering, waiting for God to be close enough that we feel at home in our own skin. But, for our part, we know that the Messiah has already come. Jesus made his appearance on our earth a long time ago, yet suffering is still very real. So, what difference did it make?

We learned through Jesus' life that he came to suffer, too. Rather than removing suffering and heartache from the world, Jesus came to walk with us through it. God also sent the Holy Spirit to empower us to be sources of comfort for each other. Rather than bringing an end to suffering, the Messiah brings a powerful presence to help us deal with the suffering. With the Messiah's coming, we have comfort, not the elimination of suffering, but One who walks with us, struggles with us, suffers with us, and holds our hearts through all the mess we face.

The Messiah ushers in the possibility that comfort and strength for facing suffering can be found in prayer and through the Holy Spirit speaking into our hearts. The comfort we need might also come from the touch of a human hand, that friend who is willing to come and stay, or the stranger who notices and speaks a kind word. While suffering is part of being human, the Messiah comes to let us know that we don't have to suffer alone.

The Messiah also comes to empower each of us to be comforters. As we lead the life of love to which Jesus calls us, we are compelled in our hearts to reach out to those who are hurting. The funny thing is that when we are willing to reach out in love, we discover that it does not cost us, but increases our connection with God and each other and further empowers us to handle our own suffering.

"Comfort, O comfort my people," your God is here! Let God walk with you. Try holding someone's hand, and you will walk through this difficult world and into the Kingdom of God, where sorrow and suffering really will fly away!

40

Prayer: Dear present God, through Jesus you have taught me that you hold me in your heart. My suffering is your suffering. Help me to open my heart to you so that I can know you are in this mess called life with me. Help me to open my heart to others so I can receive the love with which you have surrounded me. Amen.

Opening the Road
Isa. 40:3-5

Isa. 40:3-5 is the passage used in the New Testament as a prophecy of John the Baptist's ministry.[3] John the Baptist was seen as making the road to the human heart less of an obstacle for God by calling people to repentance. The mountains of self-reliance and pride were being pulled down. The valleys of shame and secrecy were being built up. The boulders of guilt and self-loathing were being crushed and used for gravel on the road. All of the obstacles that prevent us from knowing God and prevent God from knowing us were being washed away in baptism so that when the Messiah comes, he will have an open road to our hearts.

We probably still need a John the Baptist around since people are prone to rebuild the same barriers that he sought to pull down. Human beings are prone to want to hide when we feel guilty, keep secret what we think others, including God, will not think highly of, and put walls up to keep people from knowing the hard things going on in our lives. These barriers block us from receiving the love we need to get through the very crunches in life that we really need to be loved through. They prevent us from letting God in with God's loving and healing presence. If I am afraid that I won't be loved for who I really am, then I will try to present myself as what I think you want me to be, since love is what I need.

As Christians and the church, we can be the reason that people feel the need to put up barriers. If we are prone to see people as sinners who need to be changed before they are worthy, then we create a barrier to loving the person for whom they are and welcoming them into relationship. The church needs to be a love laboratory where we practice the art of loving and accepting each other for whom we really are, with all of our blemishes, uncertainties and differences. The Christian's job, according to Jesus, is to love one another (i.e. everyone, not just those like me) as Jesus loves me. Christians are not commanded to judge. Christians are not commanded to separate sheep from goats. We are only commanded to love unconditionally.

If we could learn to love, accept, welcome, and nurture every human being that God loves, just think what a powerful force Christianity could be. There would be no one who felt unwelcome and unsafe in the church. There would be no need for building barriers. We could all bring our messy selves and messy lives and find love and support for battling our problems. How beautiful it would be if any person of any race, economic background, sexual orientation, immigration status, or political persuasion could walk into a church and discover a community that loves her or him and accepts her or him the way God made them, rather than wanting to "fix" them so that they are acceptable to the group. How empowering it would be if each person could find people willing to walk with them through their struggles and questions and heartaches and let them put their own gifts to use. It takes a lot of time, energy, and investment to love people this way, but that is the stuff of which life is made.

A smooth, open road through which God can come to us and through which we can love each other is the prophet's vision in Isa. 40:3-5. The Messiah is coming to make that happen so that we can live real lives, be loved for whom we really are, and exercise the power of love in other peoples' lives to help them become the person God created them to be. Our job is to help knock down the barriers we have erected to keep others out and to knock down the barriers we have formed that prevent us from being loved.

Prayer: Dear Creator, you made me, loved me, and said that I was good, just like you did every other human being. Help me to accept myself as you have created me, flaws and all, so that I can be empowered to accept and love the people you send into my life. Amen.

Hope for the Smitten
Isa. 40:6-11

When the summer sun clears the trees and hits our flower bed, the daisies start to droop. Rather than standing tall and strong, they look fragile. After several days without rain in Georgia, the sun smites the grass, and it begins to turn crispy. A few days later it starts to brown. "All people are grass, their constancy is like the flower of the field." (Isa. 40:6)

Human beings can be smitten by life just as easily as flowers and grass are smitten by the sun. One day our loved one is here and the next day not, and we are alone. One day we have our health and the next day we can't even take care of our basic needs, having to rely on others for the things we used to do easily. One day we are paying our bills and making ends meet and the next day we are homeless. Life smites us, and we wither and fade.

The prophet was called to speak a word of hope into the fragility of life, and he said, "What shall I cry?" (Isa. 40:6) What could he speak that would make a difference in the lives of broken people. The people need a word that won't bring condemnation and despair, but hope. He searched for a word that would not put people down, but build them up. He searched for a word that would open doors for renewal rather than close doors in people's faces.

In 2018 thousands of people came to the southern U.S. border seeking to escape terrible and dangerous situations in their homelands of Central America. They sought to enter the United States through the legal avenue of seeking asylum. The United States greeted them with a fist in the face and did everything we could to increase their suffering. It is a shameful blot on America. If you were a prophet, what word could you speak to these broken, suffering people? What shall we cry?

We are like grass, easily smitten. Life can break us down and leave us hurting. Is there a word of hope? The prophet found one. "Get you up to a high mountain, O Zion, herald of good tidings." (Isa. 40:9) The good news is that God cares for those who have been smitten by life! God "will feed his flock like a shepherd; he will gather the lambs in his arms, and carry them in his bosom, and gently lead the mother sheep." (Isa. 40:11)

The good news is that while life can smite us, God never stops loving us, hurting with us, carrying us. Through prayer, scripture, the Holy Spirit, and God's people who have learned the way of love, we are touched, loved, and carried through the heartaches of life. The hardships won't go away, but we are not alone. And, when we are loved, we are much stronger and resilient.

Prayer: Dear God, my Shepherd, help me to be aware of all the ways you love me so that I don't feel alone in the dark. Help me to reach out in love to others, too, so that we can all be carried home. Amen.

Beautiful Feet
Isa. 52:7-10

I almost always start my morning prayers with a version of verse 7, "How beautiful upon the mountains are the feet of the messenger... who brings good news" (Isa 52:7) of you. I am quite memory challenged, so for me to remember this verse says that it really made an impression. To me, it is a wonderful image to picture a messenger running along the mountain, coming toward me with good news of peace, salvation, and God's presence. All of a sudden, I am not alone on the mountain. I'm no longer isolated in my hurt and despair. One is coming to be with me, and the messenger has good news.

Salvation begins with the hope of change. One has to be able to discern the possibility of change in one's situation, the possibility of release from suffering, the possibility of freedom from oppression before he or she can even begin to entertain the possibility that life can be better. The prophet envisions this messenger as bringing that possibility of hope, that possibility that life can change, to the people of Israel. No longer will they be stuck, no longer will they be alone, and no longer will there be only darkness. God is coming to bring light, presence, and love to them.

What a joy it is to see a point of light begin to shine in the darkness! When a person's heart connects with the realization that God is coming, salvation is at hand, and there is hope, then renewal becomes an option. Sometimes, all it takes is to discover that we are not alone in our suffering to move us toward life. Sometimes, the Holy Spirit whispering in our hearts can light the fire of renewal. Sometimes, it takes a hand to hold to pull us along. When stuck in suffering, despair, and darkness, the prophet says to open your eyes and look to the mountains and see the feet of the messenger who is bringing the good news of God's loving presence.

One day I took my wife, Beth, to the hospital for what was supposed to be a simple, laparoscopic surgery. She hemorrhaged and ended up in ICU on a ventilator. I was scared. She might not make it. I made a desperate call to my parents, and my Dad made the long drive into Atlanta and stayed with me till she was stable. Next thing I knew, some people from the church showed up, just in time. Then, some friends dropped by. I'm not sure I would have come out with my sanity had these people not shown up and been there for me. How beautiful are the feet of the messengers!

There are times when each of us needs to see the messenger coming. But, there are also times when we are called to BE the messenger, to bring the possibility of hope to a hurting soul, to offer a hand to hold. The beautiful thing about God's way of love is that you and I don't have to have it all together before we become the messenger. In fact, it is often our own struggle with brokenness and the hope that we have found as a result of that struggle that is the good news someone needs to hear.

When we are willing, we can set out on God's path of love, offer a hand to other people who are hurting, and be a messenger of hope. My feet can be beautiful, too, if I am willing to invest in God's broken people! It takes time. It takes energy. But, loving is the real stuff of life.

Prayer: Dear present God, thank you so much for taking my hand and heart and leading me through the darkness. Please help me to love enough to lend my hand to someone else who is hurting. Amen.

The Matter of Trust
Isa. 2:1-3

Now, we are jumping back in time some 200 years to pick up the writings of the original Isaiah, the prophet who spoke to Jerusalem from 742 to 701 (or 687) BCE.[4] This was the time when Israel had divided themselves into the Northern and Southern Kingdoms. Assyria was in the process of taking over the Northern Kingdom, leaving the small, Southern Kingdom, Judah, vulnerable to the possibility of being next.

Isaiah, with his prophet's eye, was able to discern that Judah's only hope was to pair the power and love of God with faithful living on the part of Judah's people. If he could bring these two together, there might be hope. If his people wouldn't listen and turn their hearts fully to God, there would only be disaster. So, Isaiah set about his mission of convincing the king and people to put their trust in God rather than in their own cunning. The result is some of the most beautiful passages in the Bible.

Picture Judah, a tiny little kingdom located along the trade route between Egypt and Mesopotamia, surrounded by much stronger nations who would love to control this space. Judah has just witnessed their northern brothers and sisters being taken over by Assyria. As a prophet, what word do you speak to your people?

Isaiah looks into his heart and sees not defeat, but victory. He sees God's house being established as the highest of mountains. He sees all people coming to worship and learn the ways of God. Isaiah proclaims that because God is God, God's mountain will always stand above everything else in the world. Despite what seems a hopeless situation, since in the background kings were plotting against Jerusalem, Isaiah proclaims that God is able to do that which seems impossible.

Now, there is a life lesson. When problems seem insurmountable, we need to put our trust in God. Unfortunately, for most of us, we have to totally exhaust our energy and self-reliance before we are willing to turn to trust. Isaiah knew that God is more powerful than any enemy the Israelites faced. When I can learn that God is more powerful than anything I will ever face, I can save myself a lot of anguish, stress, worry, and heartache. Trusting God seems like such a logical and simple thing to do. Yet, it is one of the ongoing struggles of the human heart.

Prayer: Dear gracious God, you formed the stars and set the orbits of the planets. Yet, I often find it hard to trust you with my life's struggles. Please place the seed of trust in my heart so that I can grow to rely on you more and not be tossed about by the winds of life's problems. Amen.

The End of Hate?
Isa. 2:4-5

In the midst of Judah's precarious situation, with kings plotting to come together to attack, Isaiah had an amazing vision of what could be possible through God. Isaiah's vision was much more than the platitude that if people will just trust God it will be OK. Isaiah is not just being a cheerleader, throwing out "Ra, Ra, Ra!" to keep people going. Isaiah's vision totally redefines the current reality. Isaiah sees a total reordering of human existence so that life is no longer about the strongest taking what they want at the expense of the weak. Isaiah sees a reality in which there are no longer haves and have nots but one people living and loving together under the banner of God's love.

This reordering of the world will take place through God establishing God's Kingdom. When people finally realize, accept, and behave as if God is the Creator and we are the creation, then there can be a chance that we will learn to live in peace. But, as long as human beings are prone to grab for power and make up reasons for wanting more than we need, we will be at odds with one another. Human beings even find it difficult to release the need for power and control in the church, where we are supposed to know that God is King and we are servants. People jockey for position, cling to the way it has always been, and will fight to the death over who is right about an issue.

As I write this, the United Methodist Church General Conference is meeting in St. Louis, Missouri, to try and find a way for the church to continue to function despite divisions over homosexuality. The most common cry is, "If they don't pick my way, I'm leaving the church!" People have beaten their bibles into swords and their hymnals into spears in order to make sure that they win the day.

What if the world could be different? What would it be like if we tried to love and nurture each other rather than going to war? What if our hearts open up to the possibility that God created all of us and loves each us with an eternal love. When God created each and every one of us, God thought, "That is good!" What if we could all gather around our Creator with love in our hearts and thanksgiving for the gift of life and realize that we are brothers and sisters all, every single one of us.

It doesn't matter if you believe just like I do. It doesn't matter the color of your skin, the language you speak, the religion you espouse, or the orientation of your sexuality, you and I are both created and loved by God. We were put here on this earth as an expression of God's love and called to love each other the way God loves us. When the human heart reorients to the reality that love is the very fabric of the universe, there is the possibility that we can beat our swords into plowshares and our spears into pruning hooks. Then, there will be no need to learn war, since we know love. Then, there will be no need to do battle to defend my position because loving you and building you up is my passion.

Isaiah foresaw a radical reordering of human existence so that love of God and love of neighbor becomes what defines us. The Messiah is coming to make that happen.

Prayer: Dear God of peace and love, help me to see that you created all that is out of love, that you love all of us here, and that in Jesus you offer me the chance to love as you love. Please breathe the reality of love into my being so that I can enjoy the wonders of life as you created it to be. Amen.

Stuck!
Isa. 7:10-13

Ahaz, the King of Judah, was in a pickle, in a jam, stuck. He knew that two kings, Rezin and Pekah, were plotting to ally themselves and attack his kingdom. Ahaz was terrified, and so were his people. He wrung his hands, he sweated, and he thought and thought, trying to come up with a way to defend himself and his people. But, he could see no options other than trying to make alliances with other kings.

Many people know what it is like to be stuck. Depression can do that, leaving a person unable to see a way out when there are options right in front of you. Depression can be like being stuck in a hamster ball that is painted black. You can see nothing and no matter how hard you try, it is always the same bleak darkness. Addiction can be that way, too. Everyone seems to have an answer to solve the problem, but the addicted person can see no hope or possibility. There are many ways we can become just as stuck and angst ridden as Ahaz. This, too, is the soil of salvation.

One day while wringing his heart over his situation, Ahaz looks up and sees Isaiah coming. "Oh no, it's that prophet that never seems to agree with me! What does he want this time?!" God has sent Isaiah with another message for Ahaz. He tells Ahaz to "Ask a sign of the Lord your God; let it be deep as

Sheol or high as heaven." (Isa. 7:11) Ahaz knew better than to take that bait! He responded with words that are hard to argue with, since Jesus used them himself,[5] "I will not put the Lord to the test." (Isa. 7:12) Ahaz knew he needed swords and spears to solve his problem, not just trust and a promise. He was sure this was a military issue that had no spiritual solution. He was so focused on his own thinking and solutions that he couldn't even entertain other options. Stuck!

How many times do we go around and around in our minds over problems, always bumping into the same obstacles? Like Ahaz, it is easy to become stuck, to not be able to see any solution other than the ones that aren't working. It is easy to overlook the spiritual issues because our problem seems to be bigger than that. Yet, it is often the spiritual path that becomes our stepping stone to resolution. Our very lives can depend on whether or not we are willing to open our eyes, minds, and hearts to the possibility that trust in God and relying on God's promise is the answer.

Prayer: Dear God of promise, help me to open my heart when my eyes can't see a way forward so that you can be my guide. Help me to trust in you when I can't trust myself. Help me to discover that in you there is always hope. Amen.

The Birth of Hope
Isa. 7:13-16

Isaiah had taken his son with him to meet King Ahaz and deliver God's message. Isaiah's son's name was Shear-jashub, which means, "A remnant shall return."[6] Isaiah's son's presence, I think, was meant to help drive home the point of the message Isaiah had for Ahaz, because the message had to do with the birth and naming of another child: "Look, the young woman is with child and shall bear a son, and shall name him Immanuel. He shall eat curds and honey by the time he knows how to refuse the evil and choose the good. For before the child knows how to refuse the evil and choose the good, the land before whose two kings you are in dread will be deserted." (Isa. 7:14-16)

While Ahaz was sweating over possible military alliances he could make to help defend Judah against Rezin and Pekah, including the potential pitfalls of such alliances, Isaiah comes with the message that Ahaz need not worry because God has the situation under control. Isaiah foresaw that Assyria would come and vanquish both kings and Judah would be spared.

The key to Isaiah's message is the sign. A young woman, or virgin, depending on the translation, will give birth to a son and name him Immanuel, "God is with us." The promise would be embodied in a child and in the child's name. Isaiah proclaimed that "God is with us" is the solution to this multinational military campaign. If Ahaz could find the courage to trust God, then Judah would be spared a military invasion plus the consequences of giving up power to any king with whom Ahaz made an alliance. In Isaiah's message this child embodies the answer to Ahaz' dilemma.

The truth of Isaiah's message, that God is our salvation and that we need to trust God with the issues in our lives, is so poignant that it grows over the centuries to the point of becoming one of the seminal texts pointing to the coming Messiah. The idea that the promise of God's love for us, God's never ending quest to win us back, could be embodied in the birth of a baby is so beautiful. The birth of a baby is a powerful statement of hope, of the miracle of life, and of the beauty of love.

As I prepare my heart to celebrate the birth of The Baby, I am overwhelmed by the power of God's coming to me as a newborn. That is so amazing, so tender, so close that my heart melts at the beauty of God's love. I don't believe there is any way God could have demonstrated God's love in a more powerful way than coming to us embodied in a baby to grow, live, love, die, and be resurrected for us. What better way is there for God to say that God is with us!

Prayer: Dear present God, thank you so much for being with me in body, in life, and in death. I need you every hour. Amen.

Interlude of Praise
Isa. 12:2

It is helpful to me to stop, take my attention off of my problems, heartaches, and the darkness in my life, and turn my attention wholly to God. Thinking about who God is, what God has done, and how many ways God has shown me that God loves me, lightens the darkness, lets loose the tightness in my heart, and helps my soul to sing.

That is essentially what Isaiah is doing in chapter 12. He pauses from focusing on the dire circumstances that his nation faces and the risks of the king making bad choices and turns his eyes solely on God. Remembering who God is and what God has done over the centuries of Israel's life with God, Isaiah's heart begins to sing of the wonders of God. Isaiah finds himself filled with adoration for God, who has saved and will save again.

Isaiah proclaims a total confidence in God that cannot be shaken. When he is able to turn his attention to God and away from his problems, he finds a deep trust that God is his salvation, and in God he need not fear: "I will trust, and will not be afraid." (Isa. 12:2) What an enviable position! Would that I could always feel that way!

I have discovered that there are times, brief moments really, when praise leads me to a sense of total trust. But, those moments seem to be fleeting. I try to remember back to them from time to time to help boost my confidence. When I think of the times that God has felt especially close, I find the tension, the fear, the anxiety in my heart relaxing a little bit. And that seems to be enough to give me hope to carry on.

As we prepare for Jesus' coming birth, perhaps we need an interlude of praise, a time when we turn our attention away from our problems and onto the amazing nature of God and how God chooses to come to us, walk with us, and suffer with us through life's toils. Isaiah gives us a life lesson by showing us the power of stopping and refocusing. God loves and cares for us so much that God comes to us in the form of the baby Jesus. If we can remember that, it will be enough to get us through the darkness.

Prayer: Dear saving God, It so often seems that life's darkness tries to swallow me up. Stress, tension, sadness, and apprehension squeeze my heart. Help me to look through the darkness and see your beautiful love. Help me to remember that you are here by my side. Only then can I trust and not be afraid. Amen.

The Well
Isa. 12:3-6

Today, we are not so familiar with wells. The vast majority of us get our water from a pipe that runs from a water tower. Some still have wells that are bored or drilled hundreds of feet into the ground. But, for most of human history, the well was the source of water, the second most urgent need for survival. In an arid country like Israel, the well is of utmost importance.

When Isaiah wrote, "With joy you will draw water from the wells of salvation," (Isa. 12:3) he grabbed my attention, as I'm sure he did the people to whom he was speaking. What a beautiful image. First of all, there is joy. Instead of bumping around in the depressing, heavy darkness of life, there will be joy, a lightness to life that lifts the spirit. Joy is the heart gift that comes with discovering that I can count on God and trust God with my life and difficulties. Joy comes when I discover the light of God's love in my darkness, when I discover that God is right there beside me to shepherd me through. It is with joy that I will draw water and drink from the well of salvation.

The well is another fitting image. The well is dug right into the very dirt, like a tunnel boring into the dark, messy stuff of life. It is not away from the grime and worms of life that I find the water of salvation, but right down in it. God does not wait for me to rise above my problems and brokenness, but comes to me in the midst of my darkness and sets the well of salvation. That is good news for me. I can start enjoying the waters of salvation now and don't have to wait till I have it all together and am just right.

Isaiah goes on to say, "Shout aloud and sing for joy, O royal Zion, for great in your midst is the Holy One of Israel." (Isa. 12:6) As I go through this Advent season, I am trying to prepare my heart to grasp this very truth. The Holy One of Israel is about to bore down into the darkness of my life to be with me. God is about to be born into my real world as the baby Jesus, not into some sanitized place where all is perfect. God is coming to walk with me in my darkness, to feel the hunger, the hurt, the stress, the loneliness, the pain, and even the death of what being human is all about. God is willing to dig down into the dirt of my life so that I can find light and joy and a hand to hold.

Prayer: Dear present God, thank you for being willing to come to me, to find me, in the midst of my life. Help me to realize that you are always there. Help me to trust you as my Shepherd so that I can walk through life with joy rather than anguish. Amen.

A Shoot Shall Come
Isa. 11:1

With one verse, Isaiah is able to give voice to the hope of all humanity in all ages. The stump. Dead. Decaying. It stands as a symbol of failures, mistakes, brokenness, and the dead end that life has hit. It stands as a reminder of the darkness that surrounds human life and as a reminder of death itself, until one sees the bud that grows into a branch.

Isaiah was apparently referring to Ahaz, the king of Judah, with this image of the stump of Jesse, implying that in him the line of Davidic Kings had become a dead stump, a dead end, finished. But, Isaiah is never one to become stuck in despair. He is always able to see a way forward with God. The power of this verse is the transformation that occurs with the shoot, the branch, the life that grows out of this dead thing. Where all appears hopeless and lost, God will bring life.

Isaiah's image of the dead stump echoes in my soul. Over the years I have felt like I was staring at a dead stump on many occasions. Beth, my wife, and I are in one of those seasons now. She is suffering from ongoing illnesses. When one improves there seem to be two more that step in, and this has been going on for over five years. We keep praying and walking around that stump looking for a shoot. So far, nothing. Will it come?

It is ironic that as I am writing this, one of my favorite bonsai trees, which I am afraid I have killed by failing to repot soon enough, is sitting on the deck as a dead stump. It is a small sugar maple that I dug up from the woods 19 years ago. It lost all of its leaves last summer, so I took it out of its pot and loosened the root ball. I have watered it and moved it in out of the really cold snaps all winter. Now, I wait. Will the shoot come?

That is Advent. Sitting surrounded by darkness, I wait and watch for a shoot to come from the dead stump. Isaiah could see that God comes to the crumbling decay of life and causes a new shoot to grow. Even in the darkness of death, God will cause the new shoot of eternal life to grow. So, I wait and watch. Soon I will see the bud of life, Jesus, born of Mary and lying in a manger.

Prayer: Dear transforming God, please come and speak life into the dead places in my soul. Let the life that lies in the manger live in my heart so that I have hope and can see the way forward. Please give me the strength to wait as I watch for that shoot to grow in my life. Amen.

A Beautiful Shoot
Isa. 11:2-5

Isa. 11:2-5 gives voice to the shape of the shoot for which Isaiah is longing. When Isaiah looks to the needs of his people, the solution he sees is a Messiah who will come to deliver, guide and nurture his people along the path of a relationship with God. Isaiah foresees the Messiah as being a person of wisdom, righteousness, faithfulness, and compassion.

For Isaiah, his people had reached the point of being a dead stump. They, particularly the king, no longer looked to God for answers to their problems, but tried to rely on their own self-sufficiency. God, almighty God, the Creator and Sustainer of the very universe, had been relegated to a small role of Saturday morning rituals, basically forgotten. Yet, the fire of faith burned hot in Isaiah, and he knew that God was not only needed, but the only solution to their strife. God would provide a shoot, new life growing out of the dead stump: a Messiah.

The Messiah will be a person of faithfulness, who is true to God, who delights in God, and who trusts God. The Messiah will be filled with the very spirit of God, and this will give him wisdom and compassion. He will wear righteousness and faithfulness like clothing. He will judge with equity for the poor and the meek, not based on what he sees or hears (i.e. the whispers and deceptions of the rich and powerful seeking their own good) but based on what is true and fair and loving.

It is uncanny how Isaiah seemed to have known the coming Messiah so well. I can't help but think of Jesus when I read these verses. As I look at the unfolding of the Messiah's life, I see that Jesus' focus was on the poor and marginalized of society. He always went to the broken, the hurting, and the outcast. If Jesus' ministry was so focused on the lowly, then perhaps he might be interested in me, too.

Advent gives me a moment to pretend. While I know that Jesus has already come, Advent gives me time to look into my heart and get back in touch with the hurts, longings, and brokenness that travel with me day by day. I search to find that for which my heart is longing. What, or whom, can fill that longing? I discover that it is not winning the lottery or power or prestige for which I yearn, but love. My heart is seeking One who will love me despite my flaws and who will walk with me through the darkness and into a better day. Like Isaiah, I sit looking into the deadness of a stump and waiting for life. That life is coming in the form of Jesus.

Prayer: Dear saving God, you created me and gave me life. Then, you recreated me and gave me new life through the gift of your Son. Please come and fill my heart with your Spirit so that light and life can overcome the darkness. Amen.

Good News and Bad News
Isa. 11:6-9

Wow! What a beautiful passage! These verses leave me feeling warm, hopeful, and joyful. In these verses, Isaiah gives an amazing vision of where the world is headed through the coming of the Messiah, and it is totally different from our current reality. Isaiah foresees a kingdom of peace and gentleness, where predator and prey come to live together in harmony.

I have seen paintings of Isaiah's vision in which the wolf and lion look gentle and calm and the sheep and calves are close by with no fear, images of beauty and tranquility. But, Isaiah was probably thinking in terms of human beings in the vision he gives. In the human world, there are definitely predators and prey. Predatory people seem to constantly be trying to take advantage of, put down, or abuse other people. Human culture just seems to be prone to lash out at the vulnerable. All over the world, even in the U. S., there are leaders and militaries doing violence to different ethnic groups in their midst, as long as the group is weak and not strong enough to defend themselves. Predator vs. prey is a real phenomenon in human culture.

When the Messiah comes and leads the world to a kingdom under God, Isaiah foresees that things will be entirely different. The beauty of Isaiah's image is that those who used to be the predators come to live with those against whom they used to lash out and there is no longer animosity, hatred, or violence. People on opposite ends of the economic, political, and religious spectrums learn to live together in peace, so much so that a child can lead them. Isaiah says, "They will not hurt or destroy on all my holy mountain; for the earth will be full of the knowledge of the Lord as the waters cover the sea." (Isa. 11:9) That is good news, but also potentially bad news.

The good news is that the Messiah is coming to bring a Kingdom in which there will be peace, joy, and love for all. The bad news is that I may not be entirely comfortable with all of the people that are present in the Kingdom. Lions, wolves, bears, sheep, lambs, and cows are all fuzzy, warm, and somewhat like me. But, who let in the asps and adders? They are different, totally different from me. They make me uncomfortable. Could God really let them in? I thought we had a spot reserved for them that kept them out of the Kingdom, but here they are!

Isaiah had the heart capacity to understand that God created all people, loves all people, and will bring all people into God's Kingdom. Isaiah saw beyond Israel's needs and realized that the Messiah, Jesus, would come to save not just Israel, but the whole world. God's Kingdom is not based on my likes and dislikes, on what I say is right or wrong, but on the overwhelming power of the love of God who created this incredible universe and all that is in it.

There is one more bit of good news. Just like the child is comfortable, happy even, playing with the adders and asps, so I will be given the capacity to love and enjoy all the people that I may have thought would make me uncomfortable. When I am ushered into the Kingdom of God, I will have the heart capacity to love all whom God loves, and the Kingdom will feel like home. Maybe that could even start today!

Prayer: Dear loving God, thank you for the hope that Messiah can totally change the world. Please start the process by working in my heart, teaching me to love as you love, so that I can enjoy the beginnings of your amazing Kingdom now. Amen.

Light
Isa. 9:2-5

I will confess, Isaiah 9:2-7 is my favorite Advent passage from the Old Testament. I love to read this passage in a darkened sanctuary while the Advent candles are being lit. This passage speaks to me of the hope of transformation. After struggling so long, I finally see, hear, discover that the transformation for which I long is not going to come from my trying harder, but from God sending Messiah to save me.

"The people who walked in darkness have seen a great light." (Isa. 9:2a) Light the first candle. The flicker begins to transform the darkness. There is light, and the light is hope. Maybe the darkness will lose its heaviness. Maybe the darkness will lift, and I will find that I am not alone. Maybe the darkness is not all that there is in life after all.

"Those who lived in a land of deep darkness—on them light has shined." (Isa. 9:2b) Light the second candle. Oooh! Brighter! The force of the light is growing. I can make out evergreen around the wreath. Life. I can begin to make out faces, eyes mostly, of people nearby, shining, peering, reflecting the light of the candles. Community.

The energy of the candles begins to transform my world. Isolation, brokenness, pain, darkness are no longer all that exist. Coming to me deep in my dark world the light reaches with its warm glow, entering my eyes and radiating my heart. Just as the candle flames flicker and dance, so my heart begins to stir. The light calls and beckons. No, life is not meant for sitting in darkness. Come, draw near, and join in the dance. My spirit shivers with delight, but holds back. Can this really be? The light is so warm and inviting. Maybe it can be. Still the light beckons and dances on.

Light the third candle. "For the yoke of their burden, and the bar across their shoulders, the rod of their oppressor, you have broken as on the day of Midian." (Isa. 9:4) I want to go to the light, but discover that I am restricted. I become aware of a pain across my shoulders. My hands are bound to some kind of pole. It never hurt before, but now I can hardly stand it. If only I could get free. How did this pole get here? Did I tie myself in or did someone else do this? Either way, it suddenly seems unfair. I need the light. I want the light. But, I can't get there. My spirit yearns for the possibility of being in the light, but my body cannot move. My only hope is that the light might come to me.

Wait. The light is getting closer.

Prayer: God of light and life, I have lived in darkness in so many ways. The light of your love beckons to me to leave my dark ways behind and live in your love. Please help me to let you come to me and bring your Light so that I might live. Amen.

The Child
Isa. 9:6

The gift of a child is such a precious thing. A new life comes into one's midst in a sudden, laborious way. No longer are there subtle or not so subtle kicks in the womb, where this life has been contained for nine months. Now, arms and legs are flailing about and there is noise, that first cry. A new person is here, and that person is a force with which to be reckoned.

The birth of my child changed my life. Suddenly, I had new responsibilities for keeping this tiny person alive. The tasks of feeding, swaddling, changing, cuddling, dressing, napping were suddenly called forth from my being. Fortunately, the love needed to make these tasks a joy was also summoned with the arrival of this baby.

My wife and I tried to heed the advice to take in every moment because the child will grow up in no time. Changes happen daily. Within a couple of weeks, the newborn wasn't newborn anymore. The child who could lift her head off of the mattress was suddenly rolling over, then crawling, then walking. Sarah, my child, took her first steps holding her mother's tennis shoes by the laces. I guess that gave her balance. At that time, I had no way of knowing what Sarah would grow to be or do. I just had love to help us get there.

Tonight is the magical night when we come together to celebrate the birth of another child, Jesus. Jesus entered Mary and Joseph's lives just like other children, with noise and flailing arms and legs. Mary and Joseph knew Jesus was destined for something incredibly special, but at that time, they could not see what Jesus would grow to be or do. Yet, somehow Isaiah, writing some 700 years earlier, was able to discern the character of this most special of babies.

Isaiah has the audacity to name Jesus some 700 years before he is born, and the names are quite large for a small baby. As Isaiah discerns that God will send the Messiah to save, Isaiah writes that he will be called, "Wonderful Counselor, Mighty God, Everlasting Father, Prince of Peace. That is a lot to lay on the shoulders of a newborn! Yet, that is exactly why this night is so magical, special, and wonderful.

Tonight we celebrate the birth of Jesus, who is very God of very God. Jesus, both fully divine and fully human, enters our world through Mary's labor pains and grows to be our Wonderful Counselor, walking with us through our broken times. Jesus, though born just like the rest of us also rises from the dead, an everlasting Savior. Jesus, though raised in the home of a carpenter, lives a life and ministry of peace, calling people to love each other no matter what their differences or divisions, not just tolerate one another but actually love each other. (Yes, I think Jesus was serious about that!)

"For a child has been born for us, a son given to us." (Isa. 9:6) Jesus, born of Mary's battle with labor and ushered into our world with angels' song, is the Messiah whom Isaiah could see coming. Jesus is God come to be with us in our grimy, hard, broken world, not just to sit with us in the misery, but to comfort, heal, and call us out into a brighter, more joyful life of love. As I think of this amazing birth, my heart fills with joy and warmth. How could God love me so wonderfully?

Prayer: Dear present God, thank you for loving me more than I love myself. Thank you for coming to me to save me. Thank you for walking with me to guide me. Thank you for lifting me up when I fall. Thank you for healing me when I hurt. Thank you for living in the midst of the mess of my life with me. Amen.

A New World
Isa. 9:7

This world is a hard place. Rocks, roots, briars, splinters all reach to tear and bruise. Life, precious life, can be snuffed out in a moment in a car or drag and bump with a heavy weight with Alzheimer's. As if the hardness of this world weren't enough, we humans are good at creating turmoil and strife, lashing out, condemning, deriding one another as if we could manage our journey on this planet without the other. Ridicule, condemnation, and bitterness can be part of a person's daily fare. Loneliness, too, is a hard thing. As I write this, there is a lone mallard swimming in the pond. While he's a beautiful duck, I feel sad, wondering where his mate is this spring morning. He calls, but no one answers.

There are soft places in the world where it is comfortable to be. The sand on the beach or gentle waves lapping in the ocean can be soft. But they can turn on me. If the day is too hot the sand can burn, and the waves can get rough, knocking me down.

In my better moments, when I am still and calm, I can imagine a softer world. I picture a world where I can count on finding comforting encouragement, where loneliness gives way to comradery, and where there is one to help me up when I fail and fall. This new world is one where condemnation flees in the light of compassion, where tearing and bruising are replaced with healing and guidance, and where understanding and acceptance squelch fear and anger. This new world is the one Isaiah sees. But, Isaiah is also able to see how we get there.

Isaiah somehow knew that God would send the Messiah into our world to usher in peace and love. A new Kingdome would be built, and it would be a softer place to live. Today is the day we celebrate that coming. Jesus' birth is the dawn of a new world that God is giving to us. Realizing that human beings cannot soften the harshness that we have created, God sent Jesus to do it for us. And, God does not do this begrudgingly, as a last ditch effort, but with zeal.

The grandchildren open Christmas presents with zeal. Paper flies and there is joy and excitement all around. I like to picture God feeling that way when Jesus was born. With excitement and energy, God enters into the process of saving humanity from ourselves. Zealously, God takes on the hard human flesh, walks the hard human road, and dies the hard human death so that you, I, and all of humanity can enter into a new life of love, peace, and joy. "The Zeal of the lord of hosts" (Isa. 9:7) has done this.

Merry Christmas!

Prayer: Dear God of love and zeal, you came to me in Jesus that I might come to you and live. Please give me the zeal to love you with all of my heart, to love my neighbor as you love me, and to enjoy the beauty of life with you. Amen.

Discussion Guide

Session I: Devotionals 1 – 7

The Coming Presence: Start off by discussing Advent as a season of watching, waiting, and preparing for the coming of our Savior. But, it's not just preparing for Jesus' birth, we are also preparing for his return, when he will establish the Kingdom of God and end human history. It might be helpful to have hymnals or copies of the hymn, "Let All Mortal Flesh Keep Silence." Ask the class members to look over the lyrics and discuss how this fits with Advent. Think about how the tune fits, as well.

Think about the first verse of this passage: "O that you would tear open the heavens and come down, so that the mountains would quake at your presence." (Isa. 64:1) In Isaiah's time, the earth was understood to be a saucer resting on pillars with a dome covering it to keep the "waters" up above from pouring down on earth. Isaiah pictures God as tearing open this dome and coming down to earth. What does it mean for the presence of Almighty God to come into our midst? How will it be uncomfortable?

Filthy Rags: Ask the class to discuss sin and how it manifests itself in their lives. How can sin be like filthy rags? Discuss Isaiah's description of sin and how it applies to today's world. What do you think of the idea that even good deeds are tainted? How does understanding sin in one's life help one be more ready for Jesus' coming?

The Birth of Hope: Focus on the image of potter and clay. What can clay do? How are human beings like clay? Ask the class to share things that we human beings cannot fix in our lives. In what ways are we like the Israelites today? How are we stuck in situations that we cannot overcome without help? One of the purposes of the Advent season is to help us realize that we need a Savior. We really can't navigate this life on our own. We need a Savior to come had help us through. Ask the class how this passage helps them to realize their need for a Savior.

Rise and Shine!: The passage for this devotional is a beautiful call to hope, a wonderful expression of how God can transform the darkness of life into a bright wonder. If your class is open to sharing, ask them to share some of the dark moments in their lives when they felt hopeless and how God might have helped them through that time. What, exactly, is hope? How does it work in our lives? In what ways do we need hope today? How do you see God at work bringing light into darkness in today's world? Are there ways we can help bring the light?

Good News Afoot: God seems to have a special concern for the lowly and downtrodden of our world.

This passage expresses that concern in a beautiful way. Have the class look at Luke 4:16-21 and talk about how Jesus' ministry lives out this passage. What does it mean for us who are not oppressed, prisoners, or poor? While we may not fall into those categories physically, we tend to all fall into them spiritually. Ask the class to discuss how this passage speaks to them personally. How does this passage bring us comfort? How does it challenge us to live?

A Mantle of Praise: Another beautiful expression of hope, this passage touches us where we struggle. Ask the class to talk about times they have grieved and mourned. What did they find helpful during these times? Does anyone recall something said that was meant to be helpful but at best seemed empty and possibly made them upset or angry? In what ways does God give us a garland instead of ashes? How does that happen? How can we be a source of hope to people who mourn? Ask people to discuss the imagery of this passage and how it speaks to their hearts.

The Gift of Garments: You could begin the discussion by asking, "What does the clothing we wear say about us? It signals whether we are set to work out, go to work, get grimy in the yard, or lounge around the house. What else does clothing do for us? Ask the class how Jesus' description of the prodigal son fits with the Isaiah passage. In what ways does this passage bring hope to broken people? In what ways does it speak hope to your life? To find hope, I have to recognize the ways I am broken. Advent is a good season for exploring that. Can you think of ways to get in touch with the broken parts of one's life? Explore the image of planting a seed in dirt and expecting life to grow. In what ways does God do that in people's lives? Ask people to share how God has brought for life out of the hardships and brokenness of their lives.

Session II: Devotionals 8 - 15

From Desolation to Delight: Isaiah writes about changing the names of Jerusalem. Managing surnames in marriage is a tricky thing, and different cultures have come up with different ways to handle it. American culture has traditionally expected the woman to take the man's surname. Ask the women of the class to share how that felt/feels. What did they feel they lost with changing their names? What did they feel positive about it? If there are couples that chose to hyphenate, how did they decide to do that? How will their children manage surnames when they marry? Names are so important. They hold our identity. Even dogs and cats know their names. Isaiah here uses the importance of the name to demonstrate the transformation that Jerusalem is about to experience. What does the change in Jerusalem's name communicate to us? If a name is the very essence of a being, then Jerusalem's very essence is changing. Is that true for human beings, too? Does God's claiming, loving, and transforming our lives change our very essence? What does it mean in a person's life to change one's name from "Mine" to "God's"?

The Wait: People tend to spend a lot of time waiting. We wait on hold on the phone, wait in doctor's offices, wait in traffic, and on and on. Ask people to share how they handle the time spent waiting. Of course, this type of waiting is just a minor irritation in life's journey. What about waiting on hard things, like health problems, financial crises, grief, divorce, and etc. How do people handle these difficult waits? What can we do to get through these dark times? What hope does this passage in Isaiah offer us? Isaiah realized that Israel had to stay connected with God and keep an eye on God's promises to survive their dark days. We can do that, too.

Harnessing the Power of Memory: The Bible is basically a memory tool, helping us to remember our relationship with God and how God has interacted with us in this world. Ask the class to remember some of the Old Testament events Isaiah might have been calling his people to summon to mind. Christians are particularly charged with remembering during

Communion. We are called to remember Jesus, his life, suffering, death, and mostly, his resurrection when we come together for Holy Communion. Ask the class to discuss whether or not remembering that Jesus appeared to the disciples after his resurrection helps them feel closer to God. It might be fun to ask the class to close their eyes and summon to memory their mountain top experiences, the times they felt closest to God. Ask the class to share how the memories made them feel. What happens if we forget these experiences?

Blooming Deserts: This is one of the passages that inspired the cover for this book and is one of my favorites. While this passage is placed in the first part, belonging to the original Isaiah, many scholars think it is actually from deutero-Isaiah, the part written after the exile. You might have a large map so that people can see how the desert is physically between Babylon and Jerusalem. Ask the class to discuss the symbolism of this geographical barrier. Ask the class if they have ever felt like there was a desert, a barrier, between where they were and where they wanted to be. How does that feel? What does the symbolism of God transforming the desert into a blooming, living place mean? How does that speak to our lives today? Has anyone had an experience like this in life?

Journeying Together: If you were in the Israelite's position of preparing to leave Babylon and return home, how would this passage affect you? Ask the class to picture themselves as packing. What would they take for the long walk back to Jerusalem? How would you feel when you hear that you are supposed to help your neighbor who is old and needs to have his stuff carried for him? What about the woman with arthritis who may need to be carried herself? The young family with twins needs help carrying a baby. This would slow your family down and make the journey harder. Would you do it, or just turn a blind eye and walk, knowing that you have a responsibility for getting your own family there? How does this passage speak to the church today? Taking my own, private spiritual journey may seem easier, but it is lifeless. Joining hands with the rest of humanity and seeking to share, serve, and walk together is the stuff of life. It seems like the Messiah said something about that, too!

The Way Home: This might be a good time to ask the class to share ways in which they have felt stuck, lost, or hopeless. It might help to open people up if you share an experience from your own life. Ask people to look at Isa. 35:8-10 and discuss what this says to them. What does it say about God's way of dealing with humanity? How does this passage speak hope to us?

Comfort: Ask people to share what comforts them. Where do they find comfort? The source may be as simple as a cup of tea or as elaborate as candles and meditation. Does it make a difference that Jesus came to walk with us in our suffering? Jesus suffered hunger, grief, betrayal, even death, so he knows what we go through. But, how does this help me? Ask the class to discuss that issue. How can we be sources of comfort for each other? Can I receive comfort if I never share my struggles with another person? To be a source of comfort for another person, that person has to feel that I won't judge them, think less of them, or give them pat answers. They need to believe that I will actually enter into the struggle with them, feel the pain with them. How do we become that type of person?

Opening the Road: Ask people to think about the barriers of which they have heard people speak who aren't in church or consider themselves nonreligious. Most of the time, it will include hypocrisy. Shortly after Notre Dame burned, I heard one nonreligious person state that he felt Christians were leaving caring for humanity up to his type while all they cared about were their buildings. Ouch! Can that be true? Is that how the world sees Christians? Think about barriers in your own church. Is there any type of person who would not be welcomed and loved on if they walked into your church? The easy answer is, "Of course not." But is that really true? Do we consider ourselves a congregation of saints or sinners? The church's mission is to open smooth roads for God to reach people's hearts with God's unconditional love. How are we doing that as a church? How am I doing that as a Christian?

Session III: Devotionals 16-22

Hope for the Smitten: Ask the class to make a list of people in today's world who have been smitten by life, who are suffering terribly. Prompt the class to think globally as well as locally. Some of the life-crushing situations in which people find themselves are hard to imagine. What word of hope do we, as Christians, we as the church, have for a hurting world. Ask the class what they think God thinks/feels about the people who are suffering. How does verse 11 speak to today's suffering people?

Beautiful Feet: Ask the class to share times in their lives when people have had beautiful feet, have brought hope and comfort to them. How did it feel when this happened? How can we be messengers of hope for other people? Talk about how we have to be willing to invest ourselves in the lives of other people if we want to bring hope. We can't do it sitting on the couch at home! The devotional talks about hope and comfort being found in relationship. What role does presence play in our finding hope? Do we really need God or another person in our lives to find hope and possibility in the midst of our suffering?

The Matter of Trust: Ask the class, "How do we learn to trust? Where does trust come from?" Who are the people you trust? Why do you trust them? What does it take for us to learn to trust God? Why do you think human beings are so resistant to trusting God? Why do we seem to prefer self-reliance to God-reliance? Trust seems to require a history of interaction to build. Perhaps we can risk trusting God with little things so that we can learn to trust with bigger things. Look at the poem at the beginning of the book. How does it speak to this issue of trust?

The End of Hate?: Isa. 2:4 is one of the most powerful images in the Bible. Ask people to share what the passage means to them. Are there areas in your particular church to which this passage speaks? What is going on in your community that needs some swords beaten into plowshares? If your group is open to the possibility, discuss the current debate over homosexuality. Why would we say it is OK for homosexual people to be in the church, but not in leadership positions? Homosexuality has been a part of all cultures throughout time, and people who are homosexual state that they were born that way and did not choose. How does this impact our understanding of this issue? You could also ask the class to discuss how Christians are to relate to people of other religions.

Stuck!: Take a moment to flesh out how Ahaz was stuck between a rock and a hard place. Facing attack, he could ally himself with other kings, who would send soldiers to help defend Judah. But, there is always a cost to that kind of alliance. Ahaz would have to surrender something, territory, control, or wealth, to secure the alliance. Ahaz was stuck because he could see no good options. Ask people to discuss how issues like depression and addiction can get people stuck. Ask the class to share situations in which they have found themselves stuck. How many times did it turn out to be a matter of trust and of opening the heart to God that proved to be the solution? In what ways can these situations that leave people feeling stuck be the soil of salvation?

The Birth of Hope: Why do you think God was so determined to give Ahaz a sign when Ahaz didn't seem to want one? Ask the class to discuss the poignancy of the sign itself. What does a baby named Immanuel say to Ahaz' situation? How does this passage speak to us of Jesus' birth? The sign was to offer Ahaz and his people hope that their land and nation would survive. What does Jesus' birth offer us?

Interlude of Praise: Perhaps the best way to approach this lesson is to ask people to close their eyes and remember the times when they have felt closest to God. What was going on in their lives at the time? How do they feel now after having taken this trip down memory lane? Is there potential in spending time remembering one's mountain top experiences and reflecting on God's love?

Session IV: Devotionals 23-29

The Well: Take a moment to discuss joy. What is it and where do we find it? Ask the class to share the things/people that bring them joy. Discuss the author's description of the well as a symbol for God reaching down into the messy darkness of our lives. How does the symbol fit with the coming birth of Jesus? Why do you think God came to us in the brokenness of our lives rather than expecting us to climb to God's level?

A Shoot Shall Come: Ask the class to discuss how the image of a shoot coming out of a dead stump is fitting for the Advent season. How does this image speak to our world today? Ask the class to share how they have experienced this very image playing out in their lives. Unfortunately for me, the bonsai tree that I discussed is dead. Can life come out of death, itself? Can we find hope and life in the midst of losing the people we love to death? How does this image speak to our times of grief?

A Beautiful Shoot: Ask the class to list events in Jesus' life and ministry that fit with Isaiah's description of the Messiah, events in which Jesus was for the poor and outcast, in which his words smote the people around him, and in which he exhibited righteousness and faithfulness. The more things change the more they stay the same! Ask the class to look at the second paragraph in the devotional and discuss whether or not any of that fits with today's world. In what specific ways can Jesus be the answer to today's problems and issues? In the last paragraph I contend that what I need most in life is love. Does this ring true with the class? If so, how is Jesus the answer to that need?

Good News and Bad News: Ask the class to share the feelings and thoughts that this passage from Isaiah evokes in them. It might be fun to pull up images of paintings of this scene to share. Ask the class to share what sort of feelings they have about the child playing over the snakes' dens. What does this image say about the church? What does it say about heaven? Is there anything we can do to make our current reality more like Isaiah's vision?

Light: This devotional is an exercise in imagination. Ask the class to picture themselves sitting in a dark sanctuary as the Advent candles begin to be lit. How does this passage from Isaiah speak to them? What does the light represent? What does the pole in the last part of the devotional represent? Ask people if they can identify with any particular parts of this devotional. Ask the class what they think of the ending of this devotional. What do you think the author was trying to say?

The Child: If your class has parents in it, ask them to remember back and share feelings they had when their child was born. Connect these with how Mary and Joseph might have been feeling. Discuss the different names that Isaiah gives to the Messiah and how they fit Jesus. Ask the class to dig out specific instances from Jesus' life and ministry that reflect these different titles. Ask the class how Jesus' birth and presence in our world affects our lives. Ask people to share what they have gained by having Jesus present in their lives.

A New World: Ask the class to share visions of what their ideal world would look like. Does it include any of the items in Isa. 9:7? How does Jesus' birth help move us toward that ideal world? What role does the church have to play in making the world in which we live closer to ideal? Ask the class to discuss what it means for God to take on "the hard human flesh." Ask the class what it means to them to realize that God is willing to walk through suffering with us. Does that help in dealing with suffering? It would be nicer if suffering were carried away, but having someone with us when we are suffering means a lot.

Endnotes

[1]The United Methodist Hymnal. Nashville: The United Methodist Publishing House, 1989. p. 626.

[2]The New Oxford Annotated Bible. Metzger, Bruce and Murphy, Roland, Editors. New York: Oxford University Press, 1991. Print. p. 866, OT.

[3]Matt. 3:3, Mark 1:3, Luke 1:76 and 3:4-6, and John 1:23.

[4]The New Oxford Annotated Bible, p. 866.

[5]See Luke 4:12.

[6]See Matt. 4:7 and Luke 4:12.

Made in the USA
Monee, IL
31 October 2023